NUMBER CRUNCH YOUR WAY AROUND

EUROPE

Joanne Randolph

PowerKiDS press™

New York

Published in 2016 by **The Rosen Publishing Group**
29 East 21st Street, New York, NY 10010

Produced for Rosen by Calcium

Editors for Calcium: Sarah Eason, Rosie Hankin, and Katie Dicker
Designer: Paul Myerscough

Art by Moloko88/Shutterstock

Photo credits: Cover: Dreamstime: Ryhor Bruyeu (top), Zoom-zoom (bottom); Shutterstock: Ivan
Bastien (back cover); Inside: Shutterstock: A.B.G. 16, 29b, Atm2003 6bl, Ivan Bastien 14tr, Greg Blok
26t, Aleksander Bolbot 24l, Burben 5t, Canadastock 6r, 11c, 28l, 29t, Bucchi Francesco 26b, Filip Fuxa
18t, Giedriius 7t, Goodcat 12l, Dave Head 21r, Patricia Hofmeester 19tl, JuliaLine 9r, Iakov Kalinin
4br, Kekyalyaynen 7r, Alan Kraft 23tl, Philip Lange 4bl, Littleny 20r, 28r, Viacheslav Lopatin 27r, Oleksiy
Mark 17tr, Martin M303 18bl, MilousSK 25r, Jaroslav Moravcik 24br, Andrei Nekrassov 14b, Gardar
Olafsson 19b, Inacio Pires 13tl, Andrei Pop 15r, Nicram Sabod 16tr, SF photo 11br, Sergey Sizov 10tr,
Stocker1970 20tr, 26l, Stockphoto-graf 1, 12r, TTstudio 5b, Maria Uspenskaya 13br, Vaclav Volrab 9bl,
XXLPhoto 22l; Wikimedia Commons: Koosha Paridel 23r, Stefg74 8tr.

Cataloging-in-Publication Data
Randolph, Joanne.
Number crunch your way around Europe / by Joanne Randolph.
p. cm. — (Math exploration: using math to learn about the continents)
Includes index.
ISBN 978-1-4994-1245-1 (pbk.)
ISBN 978-1-4994-1260-4 (6 pack)
ISBN 978-1-4994-1264-2 (library binding)
1. Europe — Juvenile literature. 2. Mathematics — Juvenile literature.
I. Randolph, Joanne. II. Title.
D1051.R36 2016
940—d23

Manufactured in the United States of America

CPSIA Compliance Information: Batch WS15PK: For Further Information contact Rosen Publishing, New York, New York at 1-800-237-9932

Contents

Europe   4

What a Continent!   6

Mountains   8

Rivers   10

The Mediterranean Basin   12

Greece   14

The Nordic Countries   16

Iceland   18

The British Isles   20

The Straits   22

The European Plain   24

An Amazing Continent   26

Math Challenge Answers   28

Glossary   30

Further Reading   31

Index   32

Europe

Europe is the birthplace of western **culture**. Europeans have influenced every **continent**, through exploration and sometimes **colonization**, in the 1500s through the 1900s. Europeans colonized the Americas, Africa, Australia, and much of Asia. Are you ready to explore this region using your best map and math skills?

How to Use This Book

Look for the "Map-a-Stat" and "Do the Math" features and complete the math challenges. Then look at the answers on pages 28 and 29 to see if your calculations are correct.

A Lot of Peninsulas

Europe is a **peninsula**. This means that it is surrounded by water on three sides. The interesting thing about Europe is that its peninsula is made up of many smaller peninsulas. Some of the larger ones are the Iberian, Italian, Balkan, Jutland, and Scandinavian peninsulas.

North Sea

Atlantic Ocean

Strait of Gibraltar

Venice, Italy

The Northern Lights can be seen in some northern regions of Europe.

Map-a-Stat

The Iberian Peninsula is the third-largest European peninsula. It has an area of around 225,000 square miles (582,750 sq km). It is made up of Portugal, Andorra, Spain, part of France, and the Gibraltar **territory**.

The Italian Peninsula is sometimes called the "boot" for its shape. The peninsula stretches for around 600 miles (960 km) from north to south.

The Balkan Peninsula includes a number of countries, such as Albania, Bosnia & Herzegovina, Bulgaria, Croatia, Macedonia, Montenegro, Romania, Serbia, Slovenia, and Moldova. It has a total area of around 257,400 square miles (666,700 sq km).

Black Sea

Mediterranean Sea

Prague, Czech Republic

DO THE MATH!

Use the information in red in the Map-a-Stat box to figure out the following challenge. How long would it take you to drive from the Po Valley at the north of the Italian Peninsula to the Mediterranean Sea in the south, if you drove at a rate of 50 miles per hour? Here is the equation to help you solve the problem.

600 miles ÷ 50 miles per hour = ? hours

Complete the math challenge, then turn to pages 28—29 to see if your calculation is correct!

What a Continent!

Europe is the world's second-smallest continent by size. It is 3.83 million square miles (9.93 million sq km) in area. It is the third-largest continent by its population, which is around 742 million.

So Many Habitats

Europe has many different **ecosystems** and **habitats** for its plants and animals. It has **tundra** and **taiga** in the far north, and forests, **grasslands**, and **pasturelands** in western and central Europe. The regions along the Mediterranean Sea have a mild **climate**, and crops such as olives and grapes are grown there.

The land around the Alps is covered in forests and grasslands.

Tuscany, in Italy, has many protected natural areas.

Map-a-Stat

Around 25 percent of the animal **species** in Europe are **endangered**. Some of this is caused by habitat loss, pollution, or hunting by people. Some is caused by competition from other species not typically from the area.

Asia and Africa both have more people than Europe. Asia's population is around 4.4 billion, and Africa's population is around 1.1 billion.

There are 50 widely recognized countries in Europe.

This hare lives in the Scottish Highlands.

DO THE MATH!

Use the information in red in the Map-a-Stat box to figure out the following challenge. The population of the world is around 7 billion. If you add the populations of the two most populated continents, Africa and Asia, how many people live in the rest of the world? Here is the equation to help you solve the problem.

7,000,000,000 people − (4,400,000,000 + 1,100,000,000 people) = ? people in the rest of the world

Karelia, an area found in both Finland and Russia, has the two largest lakes in Europe.

Complete the math challenge, then turn to pages 28—29 to see if your calculation is correct!

Mountains

Europe has many beautiful mountain ranges. The Alps are in the southern part of central Europe and run for 750 miles (1,207 km). They are known for their amazing views, lakes, valleys, and **glaciers**, and they offer some of the best skiing in the world. The Balkan Mountains run from Bulgaria to the Black Sea. The highest peak in Greece is Mt. Olympus. It was home to the gods of Greek **myths**. Other mountain ranges include the Carpathians, the Caucasus, the Pyrenees, the Apennines, and the Urals.

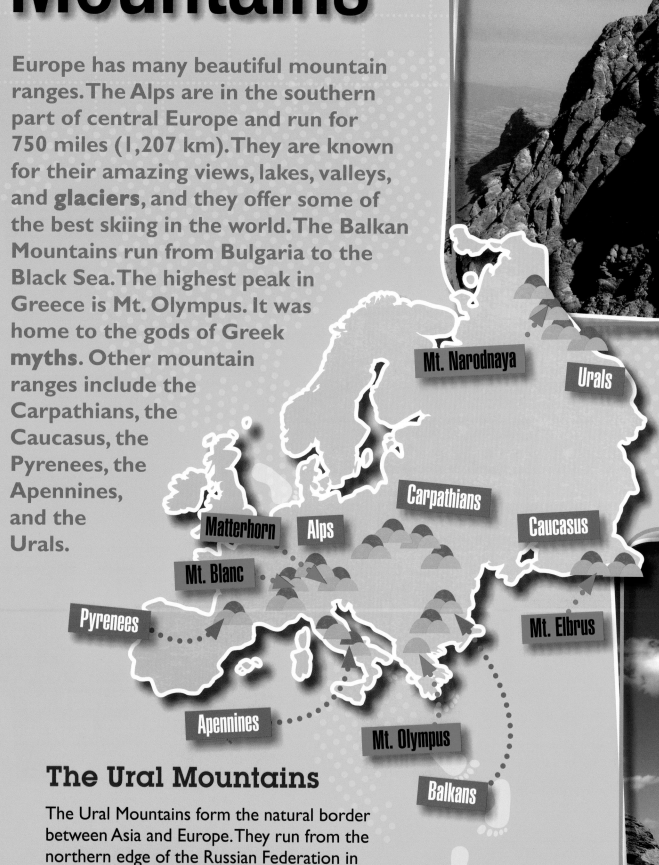

Mt. Narodnaya

Urals

Carpathians

Caucasus

Matterhorn

Alps

Mt. Blanc

Pyrenees

Mt. Elbrus

Apennines

Mt. Olympus

Balkans

The Ural Mountains

The Ural Mountains form the natural border between Asia and Europe. They run from the northern edge of the Russian Federation in Europe through Kazakhstan. They are around 1,550 miles (2,500 km) long.

Map-a-Stat

The highest point in the Alps is Mt. Blanc at 15,771 feet (4,807 m).

The highest point in the Ural Mountains is Mt. Narodnaya at 6,217 feet (1,895 m).

Mt. Olympus in Greece is 9,568 feet (2,916 m).

Mt. Elbrus is considered by many people to be the highest peak in Europe.

Mytikas is the highest of Mt. Olympus's 52 peaks.

The Matterhorn is a peak in the Alps.

DO THE MATH!

Use the information in red in the Map-a-Stat box to figure out the following challenge. How much higher is Mt. Blanc than Mt. Narodnaya? Here is the equation to help you solve the problem.

15,771 feet − 6,217 feet = ? feet higher

Complete the math challenge, then turn to pages 28—29 to see if your calculation is correct!

Rivers

Hundreds of rivers and their smaller branches, called **tributaries**, flow through the European continent to the sea. The Danube is one of the longest rivers in Europe. It flows 1,771 miles (2,850 km) from the Black Forest in Germany to empty into the Black Sea. The Dnieper and the Don Rivers both begin in the Russian Federation, part of which is also found in Asia. The Elbe starts in the Czech Republic and flows north into the North Sea.

Volga River

Rhine River

Elbe River

Don River

Dnieper River

Loire River

Po River

Danube River

The Rhine River

The Rhine and the Danube are famous for once forming the border of the Roman Empire. The river is considered to flow between 766–820 miles (1,232–1,319 km) from the Swiss Alps and empties into the North Sea. The Rhine River's course is shorter today than it once was, though. The course was changed to accommodate a number of **canals** that improved its use as a waterway.

Map-a-Stat

The Po River, at 405 miles (652 km) long, is the longest river in Italy.

The Loire River is the longest river in France. It flows 634 miles (1,020 km) from southern France into the Bay of Biscay in the northwest.

The Danube River passes Aggstein Castle in Austria.

At Nizhny Novgorod the Volga River is joined by the Oka River.

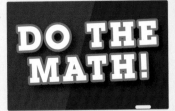

DO THE MATH!

Use the information in red in the Map-a-Stat box to figure out the following challenge. If you travel at a rate of 5 miles per hour, how long would it take you to travel down the entire length of the Po River? Here is the equation to help you solve the problem.

$$405 \text{ miles} \div 5 \text{ miles per hour} = ? \text{ hours}$$

Complete the math challenge, then turn to pages 28—29 to see if your calculation is correct!

The Rhine River forms part of the border between France and Germany.

The Mediterranean Basin

The Mediterranean Basin covers parts of Europe, Asia, and Africa. This region refers to the lands around the Mediterranean Sea. They have mild, rainy winters and hot, dry summers. Europe's Mediterranean Basin includes parts of the countries of France, Italy, Greece, Croatia, Spain, Albania, and others.

Venice, Italy, is part of the Mediterranean Basin.

Goats live happily along the rocky coasts of the Mediterranean Basin.

Mediterranean Plants and Animals

Countries around the Mediterranean have **scrublands**, **savannas**, woodlands, and some forests, especially at high ground. They are known for growing olive trees, citrus fruits, figs, cork oak, and herbs such as rosemary, thyme, sage, and oregano. Animals such as wild goats, sheep, cattle, **lynx**, and rabbits are just a few of the creatures that live there. The climate also provides good **grazing** land for **livestock**.

Map-a-Stat

Cork oak trees can live for up to 250 years. They are the source for cork used to make many items, including cork boards, wine corks, and flooring. Around 330,000 tons (299,000 mt) of cork are harvested in the western Mediterranean Basin each year, and 66 percent is made into bottle stoppers.

The Barbary macaque, a kind of monkey, lives in the Mediterranean region. In Europe, it lives in Gibraltar. There are around 230 animals living there in 5 troops, or groups.

The Mediterranean Basin, which includes land in Africa and Asia, has an area of around 810,000 square miles (2,098,000 sq km).

These cork trees have been stripped of their bark, which will be used to make cork products.

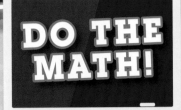

DO THE MATH!

Vineyards such as this one are common in the Mediterranean region.

Use the information in red in the Map-a-Stat box to figure out the following challenge. What percentage of cork harvested in the western Mediterranean is used to make things other than bottle stoppers? Here is the equation to help you solve the problem.

$$100 \text{ percent} - 66 \text{ percent} = ? \text{ percent}$$

Complete the math challenge, then turn to pages 28—29 to see if your calculation is correct!

Greece

Greece is a country in southern Europe. It is also known as the Hellenic Republic, and has a population of around 11 million people. Greece is at a crossroads between Europe, Asia, and Africa. It is known for its many beautiful islands. It has more than 2,000 islands but only 170 have people living on them.

Greek Geography

Greece has many mountains. Around 80 percent of its land is covered in hills and mountains. The country also has the second-longest coastline in Europe, at 8,498 miles (13,676 km).

Bulgaria

Turkey

Macedonia

Albania

Greece

Athens

Crete

Mediterranean Sea

Crete is Greece's largest island.

Map-a-Stat

The island of Crete has a population of 623,000. Euboea, the second-largest Greek island, has a population of about 207,000.

Athens is Greece's capital and largest city. It is also one of the world's oldest cities. The city alone has a population of 664,000. The population, including the city of Athens and the surrounding urban area, is more than 3 million people.

The Parthenon sits atop the Acropolis in Athens, Greece.

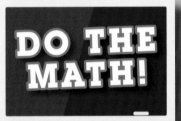

Use the information in red in the Map-a-Stat box to figure out the following challenge. How many more people live on Crete than on Euboea? Here is the equation to help you solve the problem.

623,000 people − 207,000 people = ? more people

Complete the math challenge, then turn to pages 28—29 to see if your calculation is correct!

The Metéora monasteries sit on natural sandstone pillars in central Greece.

The Nordic Countries

The Nordic countries are the nations in the northern part of the European continent. They are Denmark, Finland, Iceland, Norway, and Sweden. There are also a few territories in the Atlantic Ocean, including Greenland.

Norway is known for its fjords, which are deep inlets of sea bordered by steep hills or cliffs.

Land of Glaciers and Ice Caps

With an area of around 1.3 million square miles (3.4 million sq km), if the Nordic countries were one country it would be the seventh-largest country in the world. More than 50 percent of the land there has no people living on it. These areas are extremely cold and are covered in **ice caps** and glaciers. However, below the **Arctic Circle**, much of the Nordic coast has a surprisingly mild climate. This is because the Norwegian Current brings warm waters to the coast.

Norwegian Sea

Iceland

Sweden

Norway

Finland

Atlantic Ocean

North Sea

Denmark

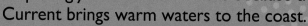

Map-a-Stat

Even if you do not include Greenland, the Faroe Islands, and the Norwegian **archipelagos** of Svalbard and Jan Mayen, the area of the Nordic countries is still huge. It covers 485,846 square miles (1,258,336 sq km). That is almost as big as France, Germany, and Italy combined, which have a total area of 502,767 square miles (1,302,163 sq km).

The Sami are the native people of the Arctic area of Sápmi, also known as Laplar. This is made up of northern Norway, Sweden, Finland, and the Kola Peninsula of Russia. The Sami's homelands have an area of around 150,000 square miles (388,500 sq km).

Stockholm is the capital of Sweden.

Some Sami people raise herds of caribou.

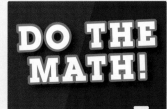

DO THE MATH!

Use the information in red in the Map-a-Stat box to figure out the following challenge. How many more square miles is the total area of France, Germany, and Italy than the total area of the Nordic countries? Here is the equation to help you solve the problem.

502,767 square miles
− 485,846 square miles
= ? square miles

Complete the math challenge, then turn to pages 28—29 to see if your calculation is correct!

Iceland

Iceland is one of the **Nordic countries.** It is an island that has an area of around 40,000 square miles (103,000 sq km). The island has only a small population, with just 326,300 people living there.

This is a hot spring in the highlands of Iceland.

Reykjavík is the capital of Iceland.

An Active Geography

Iceland sits on the mid-Atlantic ridge, which is between two **tectonic plates** in Earth's surface. The island has many active **volcanoes** and **geysers.** All this underground activity has its uses. Tourists and locals visit the many hot springs in Iceland. The steam from the hot springs is used to generate electricity, and the country's underground heat is used for heating and hot water.

Map-a-Stat

About 61 percent of Iceland's people live in and around Reykjavík.

Strokkur is a geyser in Iceland that erupts every 5 to 10 minutes.

About 85 percent of Iceland's energy comes from renewable energy sources (energy that will not run out), such as **geothermal power**.

The hot springs at Grindavík, Iceland, are a popular attraction.

Smoke and ash erupt from an Icelandic volcano.

DO THE MATH!

Use the information in red in the Map-a-Stat box to figure out the following challenge. How many times does Strokkur erupt in one hour? Here are the equations to help you solve the problem.

60 minutes ÷ 10 minutes = ? times per hour

60 minutes ÷ 5 minutes = ? times per hour

so it erupts between ? and ? times per hour

Complete the math challenge, then turn to pages 28—29 to see if your calculation is correct!

The British Isles

The British Isles are made up of the two islands of Great Britain and Ireland, and more than 5,000 smaller islands, including the Isle of Man, the Hebrides, and the Shetland Islands. The British Isles are in northwestern Europe, and their western border is the Atlantic Ocean. They are also bordered by the North Sea, the Irish Sea, and the English Channel. Great Britain is made up of three countries: England, Scotland, and Wales. The United Kingdom includes Great Britain as well as Northern Ireland.

Shetland Islands

Hebrides

Dublin is Ireland's capital and largest city.

Orkney Islands

Loch Morar

Scotland

Northern Ireland

Isle of Man

England

Lough Neagh

Severn River

Ireland

Wales

Shannon River

Thames River

Bodies of Water

The largest lake in the British Isles by area is Lough Neagh in Northern Ireland. It has an area of 151 square miles (391 sq km). Some of the other main lakes are Loch Lomond, Loch Ness, and Loch Morar, which is the deepest lake in the region. The longest river is the Shannon River in Ireland, which runs 231 miles (372 km). Great Britain's longest river is the Severn River.

Map-a-Stat

The British Isles has more than 5,000 islands, but only about 136 of these islands have people living on them.

Great Britain has an area of 80,823 square miles (209,331 sq km). Ireland has an area of 32,595 square miles (84,421 sq km). The total area of the British Isles is around 121,670 square miles (315,130 sq km).

The United Kingdom has 14 overseas territories, though some of these are disputed, which means not everyone agrees on who controls them.

Ben Nevis, in Scotland, is the highest point in the British Isles, at 4,406 feet (1,343 m).

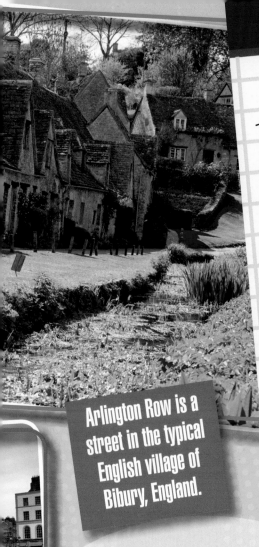

Arlington Row is a street in the typical English village of Bibury, England.

Hadrian's Wall separated England from Scotland in Roman times.

DO THE MATH!

Use the information in red in the Map-a-Stat box to figure out the following challenge. How much of the area of the British Isles is not taken up by Great Britain and Ireland? Here is the equation to help you solve the problem.

$$121{,}670 \text{ square miles} - (80{,}823 + 32{,}595 \text{ square miles}) = ? \text{ square miles}$$

Complete the math challenge, then turn to pages 28—29 to see if your calculation is correct!

The Straits

There are many straits in Europe. Straits are narrow waterways that connect two large areas of water, such as seas. One of these straits is the Strait of Otranto, which separates Italy from Albania and connects the Ionian Sea with the Adriatic Sea. The Strait of Gibraltar separates Africa from Spain. It is just 8 miles (13 km) wide at its narrowest point.

Dover Strait

Øresund

Bosphorus

Strait of Gibraltar

Strait of Otranto

the chalk cliffs along the Strait of Dover

the Strait of Gibraltar

Strait of Dover

The Strait of Dover separates Great Britain from France. The strait is at the narrowest part of the English Channel. The strait is famous as being a favorite crossing point for swimmers trying to cross the Channel. It is also famous for the white chalk cliffs along the coast.

Map-a-Stat

The Strait of Gibraltar is between 980–2,950 feet (298–899 m) deep. Many ferries cross the waterway each day. It takes each ferry about 35 minutes to cross the strait.

The Strait of Dover is about 21 miles (33 km) wide at its narrowest point.

At its narrowest point, the Strait of Otranto is less than 45 miles (72 km) across.

The Bosphorus Strait forms part of the boundary between Europe and Asia.

DO THE MATH!

Use the information in red in the Map-a-Stat box to figure out the following challenge. How long would it take a swimmer to cross the narrowest section of the English Channel, swimming at a rate of 2 miles per hour and assuming all conditions were good? Here is the equation to help you solve the problem.

$$21 \text{ miles} \div 2 \text{ miles per hour} = ? \text{ hours}$$

People use a bridge followed by a tunnel to cross the Øresund from Sweden to Denmark.

Complete the math challenge, then turn to pages 28–29 to see if your calculation is correct!

The European Plain

The European Plain is a large plain. It stretches from the Pyrenees Mountains and the French coast in the west to the Ural Mountains in the east. It has a mostly **temperate** climate, with farmland and forests, but it also has areas of **steppe**, or dry grassland. Most of the plain is less than 500 feet (152 m) above sea level.

North European Plain

Human Settlement

People tend to live where there are a lot of resources, and access to water, good farmland, and **trade routes**. In many cases, these kinds of places are found along coasts. However, because the European Plain has so many rivers running through it, it is one of the most highly populated regions in Europe.

Białowieża Forest

Sheep graze on the European Plain's grasslands.

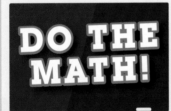

Białowieża Forest

Map-a-Stat

The European Plain is split into 2 parts, the East European Plain and the North European Plain. The eastern plain is the larger part and has an area of around 1.5 million square miles (4 million sq km).

In the west, the plain is narrow, at around 200 miles (321 km) across, but it widens to more than 2,000 miles (3,218 km) in the east near the mountains.

The European Plain is home to a very old forest that has been largely undisturbed since ancient times. It is called the Białowieża (bee-ah-wo-vay-zha) Forest. It is home to 800 **bison**, which are Europe's largest animals.

DO THE MATH!

Use the information in red in the Map-a-Stat box to figure out the following challenge. How long would it take you to hike across the narrowest part of the European Plain, walking at a rate of 4 miles per hour? Here is the equation to help you solve the problem.

$$200 \text{ miles} \div 4 \text{ miles per hour} = ? \text{ hours}$$

Complete the math challenge, then turn to pages 28–29 to see if your calculation is correct!

European bison

An Amazing Continent

Europe is an amazing continent, with Arctic tundra, mountains, beautiful forests, and plenty of beaches along its coasts. It also has many wonderful cities, such as Prague in the Czech Republic, and Dublin in Ireland, that mix their long history with modern culture. Tourists from around the world visit Europe to see its countryside and to explore the architecture, art, and culture of its many cities.

Madrid is Spain's capital.

London

Paris

Dublin

Prague

Madrid

Rome

The Eiffel Tower is a symbol of Paris, France.

London is the UK capital.

Wonderful Cities

Some of the most famous and visited of Europe's cities are London, Paris, and Rome. London, the capital of the United Kingdom, has a history that is almost 2,000 years old. Today, London is a busy city and one of the leading financial centers of the world. Paris is the capital of France. The city's **metropolitan area** has a population of around 10 million people. It is known for its beautiful buildings and excellent food. Rome, the capital of Italy, is a modern city with an ancient history. Many ancient ruins, such as the Colosseum, are reminders of ancient Roman civilization. The city has architecture from many other eras in history, as well.

Map-a-Stat

London's metropolitan area has a population of 8.3 million people.

area is about 6,590 square miles (17,069 sq km) larger than the city.

Paris has an area of around 40 square miles (105 sq km), though the city's metropolitan

It is thought that the Colosseum, a stadium built in Rome around AD 70, could hold 50,000 people.

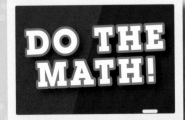

Use the information in red in the Map-a-Stat box to figure out the following challenge. What is the size of Paris's city and metropolitan area combined? Here is the equation to help you solve the problem.

$$40 \text{ square miles}$$
$$+ \ 6{,}590 \text{ square miles}$$
$$= \ ? \text{ square miles}$$

Complete the math challenge, then turn to pages 28—29 to see if your calculation is correct!

the Colosseum, Rome

Math Challenge Answers

You have made it through the math exploration! How did your math skills measure up? Check your answers below.

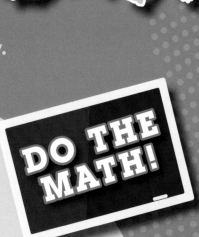

Page 5

600 miles ÷ 50 miles per hour = 12 hours

DO THE MATH!

Page 7

7,000,000,000 people – (4,400,000,000 + 1,100,000,000 people) = 1,500,000,000 people in the rest of the world

Page 9

15,771 feet – 6,217 feet = 9,554 feet higher

Page 11

405 miles ÷ 5 miles per hour = 81 hours

Page 13

100 percent – 66 percent = 34 percent

Page 15

623,000 people – 207,000 people
= 416,000 more people

Page 17

502,767 square miles – 485,846 square miles
= 16,921 square miles

Page 19

60 minutes ÷ 10 minutes = 6 times per hour
60 minutes ÷ 5 minutes = 12 times per hour
so it erupts between 6 and 12 times per hour

Page 21

121,670 square miles –
(80,823 + 32,595 square miles)
= 8,252 square miles

Page 23

21 miles ÷ 2 miles per hour = 10.5 hours

Page 25

200 miles ÷ 4 miles
per hour = 50 hours

Page 27

40 square miles
+ 6,590 square miles
= 6,630 square miles

Glossary

archipelagos Groups of islands.

Arctic Circle An imaginary line encircling the northernmost areas of the Earth.

bison A large wild mammal, similar to an ox.

canals Man-made waterways.

climate The kind of weather a certain area has.

colonization The settling of new land and the claiming of it for the government of another country.

continent One of Earth's seven large landmasses.

culture The beliefs, practices, and arts of a group of people.

ecosystems Communities of living things and the surroundings in which they live.

endangered Describing a species that is in danger of dying out.

geothermal power Power created by using steam from Earth's underground heat.

geysers Hot springs that sometimes shoot out jets of hot water or steam.

glaciers Large masses of ice that move down mountains or along valleys.

grasslands Large areas of land covered by grass.

grazing Eating grass.

habitats The surroundings in which plants and animals naturally live.

ice caps Large, thick sheets of ice covering areas of land.

livestock Farm animals reared by humans.

lynx A type of large, short-tailed wild cat.

metropolitan area A very large, heavily populated urban area, including all of its suburbs.

myths Stories passed down in a particular culture. Many myths explain how the world began and why it is the way it is.

pasturelands Grasslands used by animals for grazing.

peninsula An area of land surrounded by water on three sides.

savannas Areas of grassland with few trees or bushes.

scrublands Areas of low trees and bushes.

species A single kind of living thing. All people are one species.

steppe An area of dry open grassland.

strait A narrow waterway that connects two larger bodies of water.

taiga A forest with fir, spruce, or other types of trees with cones and needlelike leaves. Taiga often starts where the frozen tundra ends.

tectonic plates The moving pieces of Earth's crust, the top layer of Earth.

temperate Not too hot or too cold.

territory A particular area of land that belongs to and is controlled by a country.

trade routes Routes along which people buy and sell goods.

tributaries Small rivers or streams that flow into larger rivers.

tundra A cold, treeless plain with permanently frozen soil.

volcanoes Openings in Earth's crust through which ash, gases, and melted rock are forced out.

Further Reading

Books

Aloian, Molly. *Explore Europe* (Explore the Continents).
New York, NY: Crabtree Publishing, 2007.

Gibson, Karen Bush. *Europe* (The Seven Continents). Mankato,
MN: Capstone Press, 2006.

Hirsch, Rebecca. *Europe* (Rookie Read-About Geography).
New York, NY: Scholastic Press, 2012.

Lonely Planet. *Europe: Everything You Ever Wanted to Know*
(Not for Parents). Oakland, CA: Lonely Planet, 2013.

Newman, Sandra. *True Europe* (True Books: Geography).
Danbury, CT: Children's Press, 2009.

Websites

Due to the changing nature of Internet links, PowerKids Press has
developed an online list of websites related to the subject of this book.
This site is updated regularly. Please use this link to access the list:
www.powerkidslinks.com/me/europe

Index

A
Albania, 5, 12, 14, 22
Alps, 6, 8–10
Andorra, 5
animals, 6–7, 12–13, 17, 25
Apennines, 8
Arctic, 17–18, 26
Asia, 4, 7–8, 12–14, 23
Athens, 14–15
Austria, 11

B
Balkan Mountains, 8
Balkan peninsula, 4–5
Bosnia & Herzegovina, 5
British Isles, 20–21
Bulgaria, 5, 8, 14

C
Carpathians, 8
Caucasus, 8
climate, 6, 12, 16, 24
Crete, 14–15
Croatia, 5, 12
Czech Republic, 5, 10, 26

D
Danube River, 10–11
Denmark, 16–17, 23
Dnieper River, 10
Don River, 10

E
Elbe River, 10
European Plain, 24–25

F
Finland, 7, 16–17
France, 5, 11–12, 17, 22, 26–27

G
Germany, 10–11, 17
Gibraltar, 4–5, 13, 22
glaciers, 8, 16
Greece, 8–9, 12, 14–15
Greenland, 16–17

H
habitats, 6–7

I
Iberian peninsula, 4–5
Iceland, 16, 18–19
islands, 14–15, 17–18, 20–21
Italian peninsula, 4–5
Italy, 4–6, 11–12, 17, 22, 27

J
Jutland peninsula, 4

K
Karelia, 7
Kazakhstan, 8

L
lakes, 7–8, 20
Loire River, 10–11

M
Macedonia, 5, 14
Montenegro, 5
mountains, 6, 8–10, 14, 24–26
Mt. Blanc, 8–9
Mt. Elbrus, 8–9
Mt. Narodnaya, 8–9
Mt. Olympus, 8–9
Mytikas, 8–9

N
Nordic countries, 7, 16–19, 23
North Sea, 4, 10, 16, 20
Northern Lights, 5
Norway, 16–17

P
peninsula, 4–5, 17
Po (River and Valley), 5, 10–11
Portugal, 5
Prague, 5, 26
Pyrenees, 8, 24

R
Rhine River, 10–11
Romania, 5
Russian Federation, 7–8, 10, 17

S
Scandinavian peninsula, 4
Serbia, 5
Slovenia, 5
Spain, 5, 12, 22, 26
Strait of Dover, 22–23
Strait of Gibraltar, 4, 22–23
Sweden, 16–17, 23

T
Turkey, 5, 14

U
Ural Mountains, 8–9, 24

V
Volga River, 10–11